T0315888

MEMORY LANE
NEWARK
AND DISTRICT

Newark Advertiser

MEMORY LANE
NEWARK
AND DISTRICT

JOHN WEST

DB PUBLISHING

First published in Great Britain byThe Breedon Books Publishing Company Limited
Breedon House, 44 Friar Gate, Derby, DE1 1DA. 1999

This paperback edition published in Great Britain in 2015 by DB Publishing, an imprint of
JMD Media Ltd

© Newark Advertiser Co Ltd, 2001

All Rights Reserved. No part of this publication may be reproduced, stored in a retrieval system,
or transmitted in any form, or by any means, electronic, mechanical, photocopying,
recording or otherwise without the prior permission in writing of the copyright holders, nor
be otherwise circulated in any form or binding or cover other than in which it is published
and without a similar condition being imposed on the subsequent publisher.

ISBN 978-1-78091-509-8

Printed and bound in the UK by Copytech (UK) Ltd Peterborough

Contents

Introduction

Every community assumes it is at the centre of the universe. Newark and the surrounding district make an evident claim to fame.

Darwin came from Elston. Cranmer was born at Aslockton. Whittle perfected the jet engine at Cranwell. Gonville Bromhead of Rorke's Drift fame was from Thurlby. Lord Hawke, the great Yorkshire cricketer, attended Newark's Magnus Grammar School.

William Nicholson, the painter, was Newark born. Sir Donald Wolfit, last of the great actor-managers, was a son of Balderton. Lawrence of Arabia regularly played snooker at Newark Town Club during his RAF days.

Admiral Robert Sherbrooke, the Royal Navy VC, lived at Oxton. Colonel Sam Derry, who ran the Rome Escape Line in World War Two, was Newark's most decorated soldier. The famous names are varied. The list is long.

Newark's history, including a significant role in the Civil War, forms a proud story. Shakespeare's 'smug and silver Trent' makes common connection for the area with its emphasis on farming, coal and engineering.

Another important link since 1854 has been the *Newark Advertiser*. The newspaper faithfully records the area's happenings as the years unravel, latterly with a greater emphasis on pictures.

Colour photographs add a lively dimension to the scene and in this book, compiled by *Advertiser* chief photographer John West, a flavour of what makes Newark special comes into sharp focus.

Much has been told about the place and its people, but it was Caunton's 19th-century rosarian Dean Hole who said it all when he opened Newark castle gardens in May 1889. 'It may have been the Eltavona of the Romans, or the Sidnacester of the Saxons, but it is dear old Newark to me.'

R. W. K. P.

A Flavour of the Past

Kirkgate, Newark, dominated by the Church of St Mary Magdalene. (*01/Neg. 23164*)

Scenes from the Newark Parish Church in 1965. The Town Hall graces the market place, along the skyline can be seen the power station at Staythorpe. *(02/Neg. 15183b)*

Wilson Street with its terraced housing before Morrison's supermarket was built at the junction of King's Road and Slaughterhouse Lane. *(04/Neg. 15183d)*

An aerial view of Newark market place with its rows of stalls, dominated by the Parish Church and surrounded by the many streets of Newark. *(05/Neg. 31478-8)*

A typical Newark market scene taken in 1952. *(07/Neg. 1467-2)*

The centre of Newark in 1952, with the Town Hall overlooking the busy market place. *(06/Neg. 1417-5)*

Stodman Street showing Marks and Spencer, the Royal Oak public house and Farrand's grocery store in 1959. *(08/Neg. 7763)*

The Old Governor's House at 24 Stodman Street is one of Newark's grandest ancient buildings. The 16th-century house was the home of Newark's governors in the years 1643-6 at the time of the Roundhead siege on the Royalist-held town. It was also used by King Charles I during the Civil War. *(09/Neg. 37402)*

Pictured in 1964 – Ye Olde White Hart dating from the 14th century, situated in the south-east corner of Newark market place. *(10/Neg. 21698)*

One of Newark's oldest businesses, the bacon shop situated in the market place at the corner of Bridge Street – a familiar sight for the past 90 years. *(11/Neg. 27502)*

An 18th-century building at 12/13 Market Place, Newark. *(12/Neg. 27502A)*

The busy scene at the Beaumond Cross junction in 1957 where cyclists appear to out-number motor vehicles. *(13/Neg. 6199)*

A barge moored at the riverbank under the shadow of the Corn Exchange in 1970. *(15/Neg. 23279-29)*

Jallands Row taken in 1958 after
the cottages were revamped.
(14/Neg. 7288)

Every Wednesday everything from marrows... *(17/Neg. 38089-1)*

to wardrobes... *(18/Neg. 38089-8)*

to plants… *(19/Neg. 38089-10)*

…and lawn mowers go under the auctioneer's hammer at Newark Town Wharf attracting bargain hunters from far and wide. *(20/Neg. 38089-4)*

Erected as a memorial for the Viscountess Ossington's late husband, this impressive building beside the town wharf was built in 1882 as a coffee house. *(16/Neg. 37810-1)*

The Kiln Warehouse beside the River Trent in 1970, now the headquarters of British Waterways. *(21/Neg. 23279-21)*

Kelham Hall, designed by Sir Gilbert Scott, replaced an earlier structure destroyed by fire in the late 1850s. It is the former home of the Society of the Sacred Mission – a theological college – now the Newark and Sherwood District Council headquarters. *(22/Neg. 29652-12)*

The timber-framed Saracen's Head Hotel, Southwell, where King Charles I spent his final hours of freedom before surrendering to the Scots. *(23/Neg. 39332)*

The Fifties

The annual New Year social held by The Grandfathers' Club at Newark's London Road Congregational Schoolroom in January 1950. *(24/Neg. 277)*

Students at Brackenhurst Agricultural College, Southwell, on a practical course in hedge laying in February 1950. *(25/Neg. 282)*

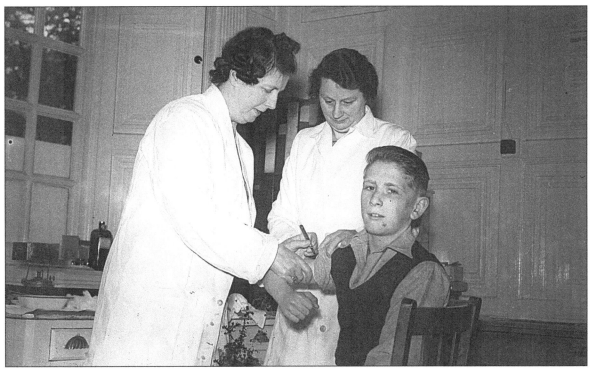

Trevor Cumberland (13) of New Street, Newark, was one of 100 people vaccinated against smallpox in 1950 before travelling to Glasgow to see an England football international. *(26/Neg. 360)*

Crowds line the riverbank to watch Newark's Regatta in June 1950. *(27/Neg. 454-8)*

The eight finalists in the Ransome and Marles Band contest to choose the 1950 Carnival Queen. *(28/Neg. 564-a)*

The Thurgarton Harvest Queen, Kathleen Oakley (12), with her attendants in October 1950. *(30/Neg. 623)*

Miss Jean French (23) a cashier at Newark Egg Packers Ltd, winner of the carnival. *(29/Neg. 564-b)*

Members of Newark Operatic Society rehearse one of the choruses in *The Pirates of Penzance* presented at the Technical College in December 1950. *(31/Neg. 628)*

Two of the characters in *The Pirates of Penzance*, Mr R. Bradbury, the Pirate King, and Mr N.E. Kirkman, one of the pirates. *(32/Neg. 718)*

23

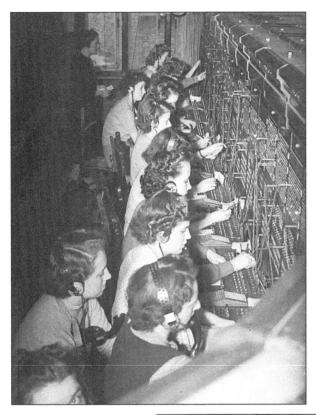

Lt-Col. W. Bush gives the Mayor (Alderman A.C. Whomsley) a carved replica of the REME badge with an engraved plate to recognise the unit's appreciation of Newark people's kindness to them in November 1950. *(34/Neg. 659)*

The switchboard operators at Newark's busy telephone exchange in October 1950. *(33/Neg. 631)*

Mr Eric Ashton, of the Brooks Motor Co, Newark, completed the first leg of the *Daily Express* car rally from Harrogate to Southend over two days. He covered over 1,300 miles in his Ford Prefect saloon in November 1950. *(35/Neg. 663)*

There was a large crowd in Appletongate when Santa Claus arrived at Henri's. He entered the premises by ladder, and then spoke to children down the chimney in November 1950. *(36/Neg. 668)*

More than 60 members of Messrs Bainbridge's staff, Newark, were treated to a dinner at The County Hotel by the firm in November 1950. *(37/Neg. 677)*

The Newark branch of the National Farmers' Union's ball at the Town Hall Butter Market was attended by 370 guests in November 1950. *(38/Neg. 690)*

Ex-servicemen march behind their associations' standards from Newark's London Road car park to the war memorial during the town's remembrance parade in November 1950. *(39/Neg. 694-6)*

Southwell's ex-servicemen leave the Minster after their remembrance service in November 1950. *(40/Neg. 694-10)*

The Southwell Red Cross detachment parades for its annual inspection in December 1950. *(41/Neg. 712-2)*

Almost 500 Newark people queued at 6.30am for their 20lbs allocation of coke at Newark Gasworks in 1951. By 8am 200 people were still waiting. *(42/Neg. 755-1)*

Newark firemen held a family party in the rest room at Newark Fire Station in 1951 at which 100 guests were present. *(43/Neg. 760-5)*

Dr P. Kinmont, JP, president of the Newark Caledonian Society, addresses the haggis at the Burns Night celebration dinner at the Robin Hood Hotel in 1951. *(44/Neg. 784)*

The four finalists in the Miss Newark contest in 1951. They were Kathleen Godfrey of Barnby Lane, Balderton, Joy Harbour of Milton Street, New Balderton, Dorothy Hillier of Rose Dean, Girton and Elizabeth Spurr of Barnbygate, Newark. *(45/Neg. 859)*

Winner of the Miss Newark title in 1951 was Elizabeth Spurr and she still reigns… *(46/Neg. 995-2)*

The new vicar of St Leonard's Church, Newark, the Revd Bernard Hill (left), is congratulated by the assistant Bishop of Southwell, Bishop J.R. Weller, after his induction in 1951. *(47/Neg. 874)*

Major-General P.N. White, Colonel of The Sherwood Foresters, inspecting men of the 8th Battalion in Newark market place after the St George's Day service in 1951. *(48/Neg. 891)*

In front of the grandstand at the 1951 Newark Agricultural Show are: front (left to right) Col F.G.D. Colman (judge), Mr Ernest Knight, Mr H.D. Cherry-Downes (vice-president), Mr E.W. Ward, Lt Col H.L.V. Beddington (president); back, Mr H.A.D. Cherry-Downes and Mrs H.D. Cherry-Downes. *(49/Neg. 922)*

A scene from Newark's Festival of Britain production of *Merrie England* which was presented in the grounds of Newark Castle in 1951. *(50/Neg. 980-5)*

The procession along Appletongate during Newark Carnival in 1951. *(51/Neg. 981-25)*

Members of the Ransome and Marles Works Band celebrate in Newark market place after winning the 99th Belle Vue brass band contest in 1951. *(52/Neg. 1081-4)*

Ransome and Marles' successful bowling team in 1951. *(53/Neg. 1095-1)*

The ceremony of the reading of the proclamation of Queen Elizabeth II in February 1952 was performed three times in Newark at the Town Hall, Beaumond Cross and Beastmarket Hill. A large crowd gathered in front of the Town Hall to listen to the proclamation read by the Mayor of Newark, Councillor J.A. Markwick, from the Town Hall balcony. *(54/Neg. 1258-3)*

The Mayor of Newark, Councillor J.A. Markwick, prepares to read out the Proclamation of Queen Elizabeth II on the balcony of Newark Town Hall. Town Clerk, Mr J.H.M. Greaves MA, the Mayor's Officer, Mr T. Turngoose DCM, and the Town Crier, Mr H. Hall, who has the proclamation stool, traditionally used for these occasions, ready for the Mayor to stand on. *(55/Neg. 1258-34)*

The Town Clerk, Mr J.H.M. Greaves reading the proclamation of Queen Elizabeth II at Beaumond Cross, Newark, whilst standing on the proclamation stool. *(56/Neg. 1258-12)*

The Town Clerk then repeated the process at Beastmarket Hill in the shadows of Newark's ancient castle. *(57/Neg. 1258-29)*

The party at Collingham Row when the Mayor and Mayoress of Newark, Dr Denys Hine and Mrs H.F. Hine, joined the residents in a celebration of the coronation. *(58/Neg. 1922-3)*

Bunting stretched out between the cottages in Collingham Row for their coronation party. *(59/Neg. 1922-13)*

Children from Newark's Hawtonville estate were in festive mood at their party in the Broadway Hotel. *(60/Neg. 1921)*

Clumber Avenue and Cavendish Avenue held a street party. The guest of honour was Councillor Mrs E. Yorke. *(61/Neg. 1939)*

Residents of Caunton choose books from the Nottinghamshire County Council mobile library in 1952. *(62/Neg. 1299-1)*

The mobile library van. *(63/Neg. 1299-2)*

Newark Rowing Club's Jim Woodman (18) is congratulated by his mother after winning the Devon Trophy at Newark Regatta in 1952. It was the first win by a member of the club at the Newark event since 1949. *(64/Neg. 1433)*

Members of the 6th Notts Platoon 307 Battalion Territorial Women's Royal Army Corps at Bowbridge Camp in 1952. They are, left to right, back: Pte W. Parr, Pte J. Yarnell, Pte M.R. Robins, Pte S. Tyers, Pte M.M. Spencer; front: Sgt M. Scott, Lt M. Allen, Capt. N. Lupton, Lt D. Jessup, L/Cpl D.J. Parr. *(65/Neg. 1533)*

Competitors in a cycle reliability trial organised by Newark Area Local Road Safety Committee in 1952. (*66/Neg. 1580*)

The first customer of a WVS bedside shopping service launched at Newark Hospital in May 1953 was the matron, Miss E.S.R. Beamish. The trolley shop was manned by Mrs P. Wetherill (left) and between them is Mrs R.C. Anderson, the hospital canteen organiser. (*67/Neg. 1902*)

Members of Newark and District Amateur Radio Society who took part in the Radio Society of Great Britain National Field Day at Dry Doddington in 1953. *(69/Neg. 1953)*

British Legion standards are paraded into Newark Parish Church in 1953 during the Legion's county rally. *(70/Neg. 1972-3)*

Firemen stationed at Newark in 1953 clean one of their engines between calls. *(71/Neg. 2078)*

The Newark and District Civil Defence Contingent's new permanent headquarters was opened on Queen's Road, Newark, by Mr S.W. Briggs, Principal Regional Officer for the Home Office, in 1953. He is inspecting a Civil Defence exhibition with, left, Mr F. Rudder, Chairman of the County Council Civil Defence Committee. In the background is Mr G.S. Christian, rescue instructor at the county Civil Defence HQ at Rufford Abbey. *(72/Neg. 2145)*

Two 1953 shopkeepers, Mr E.W. Lees of the Newark tobacconist firm whose shop was part of the Governor's House premises… *(73/Neg. 2157-A)*

…and Mr S.G. Porter of Porters the grocers, one of Newark's oldest businesses. *(74/Neg. 2157-B)*

43

A lorry carrying sugar beet along London Road collided with another lorry outside Newark Hospital in 1953. The sugar beet was bound for the Kelham sugar factory. *(75/Neg. 2214)*

A team of 28 men, women and boys dug more than 300sq yds. of a field in less than half an hour in Britain's first digging match held at Collingham in 1954. *(76/Neg. 2241)*

Newarkers enjoy the town's annual May Fair held on Tolney Lane in 1954. *(78/Neg. 2416-7)*

The bells of Newark Parish Church are lowered before being taken to Loughborough to be re-tuned in 1954. *(77/Neg. 2294)*

Newarkers flocked in their hundreds to see the Deputy Mayor, Dr Hugh Denys Raymond Hine, marry Miss Elizabeth Anne Burgass in Newark Parish Church in 1954. *(79/Neg. 2436-5)*

Newark School of Ballroom Dancing medal winners in 1954. *(80/Neg. 2489-2)*

Maypole dancing by children at Averham's garden fete in 1954. In the background is the village church. *(81/Neg. 2494)*

Newarkers stand in the rain waiting for coaches to take them on their annual holiday to the coast in 1954. *(82/Neg. 2512)*

A parade of officers in the courtyard of Newark Police Station in 1954. *(83/Neg. 2523)*

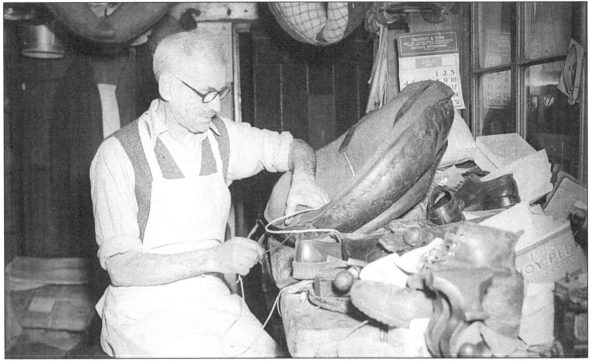

Mr W. Pridmore (72) of Main Street, Collingham, repairs an agricultural horse collar. He was one of Britain's few remaining craftsmen saddlers in 1954. *(84/Neg. 2536)*

In 1954 the Mayor of Newark, Cllr G.R. Walker, visited Newark Battalion Home Guard at Cafferata's pits and is seen eyeing up a target in the sights of a Sten gun. (*86/Neg. 2595-8*)

Also in 1954 Mr Bartholomew Waite (70) at his smithy in North Collingham. *(85/Neg. 2535)*

Sir George Kenning, JP, of Sheffield (left), waits to tap the foundation stone of the new Hawtonville Methodist Church and youth centre into place in 1954. Lowering the stone is Mr C. Bond while the general foreman, Mr L. Ingleton, guides it into position. *(87/Neg. 2606)*

In 1954 the postmistress of Shelton, Mrs J. Sentence, had to carry water in a bucket 50 yards from the village pump. The water had to be boiled before drinking. *(88/Neg. 2703)*

Children building an igloo in Fountain Gardens as Newark saw the first snowfall of the winter in 1955. *(89/Neg. 2816)*

The view from Tolney Lane towards Newark Castle during floods. *(90/Neg. 2921-13)*

Roofs of caravans peep out from the flood water near the Britannia Inn at Farndon. *(91/Neg. 2921-7)*

After 30 months on the housing list, Mr and Mrs E. Jackson were the first tenants of Newark's new maisonette homes in St Mary's Gardens, Hawtonville, in 1955. Mr and Mrs Jackson are showing the Mayor of Newark, Alderman G.R. Walker, their new gas cooker. *(92/Neg. 4023)*

The wreckage of a Provost trainer in which an instructor and his pupil were killed when the plane came down in Park Springs Wood, Caunton, in 1955. *(93/Neg. 4033)*

The instant when a Vulcan bomber disintegrated in the air. The picture was taken by David Midworth, an 18-year-old Ransome and Marles employee, at RAF Syerston's Battle of Britain Week flying display in 1958. The four crew and three people on the ground were killed. *(94/Neg. 7377-2)*

Planting potatoes on Mr R.K. Walker's farm at Averham in April 1956. *(95/Neg. 4295-5)*

Members of Newark WVS Darby and Joan Club before boarding four buses for their outing to Cleethorpes in 1956. *(96/Neg. 4388)*

The forecourt of W. Donald Ltd of Newark when petrol rationing was introduced in 1956. Private motorists had a basic monthly allowance of 200 miles and supplementary allowances for essential purposes. *(97/Neg. 4647)*

The foundation stone of the first Anglican church to be built in Newark in the 20th century was laid by Mr H.J.H. Lamb of Kettering in December 1956. This new church on Boundary Road replaced Christ Church in Lombard Street in 1957. On the left is the Bishop of Southwell, Dr Russell Barry. *(98/Neg. 4677)*

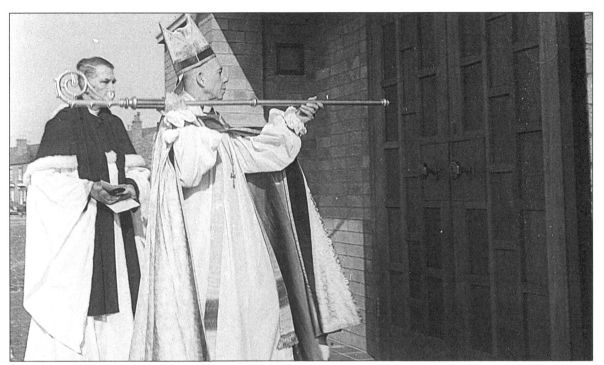

The Bishop of Southwell knocks three times on the new church's west door with his pastoral staff during the consecration of Newark's Christ Church in 1958. *(99/Neg. 7084)*

On board the tug, *Friar Tuck*, at Newark Wharf are the British Waterways men who took part in a dramatic river rescue of a man from Cromwell Weir in 1957. They are, left to right, waterways inspector Jack Bradley who organised the rescue, dredger captain Thomas Booth who made the final rescue, and skipper Jim Thompson. *(100/Neg. 4900)*

A view from the grandstand showing the parade of prize-winning cattle at Newark Agricultural Show in 1957. *(101/Neg. 4919-34)*

The crowd at the 1957 show. *(102/Neg. 4919-24)*

Neville Simpson and Zenia Smith rockin' 'n' rollin' at the Ideal Cinema, Southwell, in 1957. *(103/Neg. 4937-14)*

Newark's first woman mayor, Mrs K.A. Quibell, JP, takes a traditional sip of punch from the Loving Cup at the reception at Newark Town Hall which followed the annual Mayor's Sunday church service in 1957. In the centre is Lt-Col. G.H. Vere-Laurie DL JP, High Sheriff of Nottinghamshire. *(104/Neg. 4969-8)*

The six finalists in a Newark RAF Association beauty competition, which was judged during the RAFA Battle of Britain dance in Newark Town Hall in September 1957 were, left to right, Marlene Lambert, Pamela Parkes, Alma Quant, Maureen Cross, Lynn Goode and Ann Radford. *(105/Neg. 5034-2)*

A crowd of about 1,000 watched the ceremony of Beating the Retreat performed by the 1st Battalion Scots Guards, when they called at Newark on their way to the Edinburgh Festival in 1957. *(106/Neg. 5075)*

The Mayor of Newark, Councillor K.A. Quibell, takes the salute during the Battle of Britain march past in Newark Market Place in 1957. Also on the dais was the officer commanding RAF Winthorpe, Group Capt. A. Pike, OBE. Four flights of officers and men from RAF Winthorpe, the Newark Air Training Corps and members of the Newark Branch of the RAFA took part in the parade. *(107/Neg. 6005-2)*

Newark Town Band made its first public appearance in 1958 in front of a full house at the Savoy Cinema with a 30-minute selection of light and popular music. *(108/Neg. 7083)*

Mr Jack Baggaley's butcher's shop in Long Bennington after a lorry smashed into the front of it in 1958. (*109/Neg. 7101*)

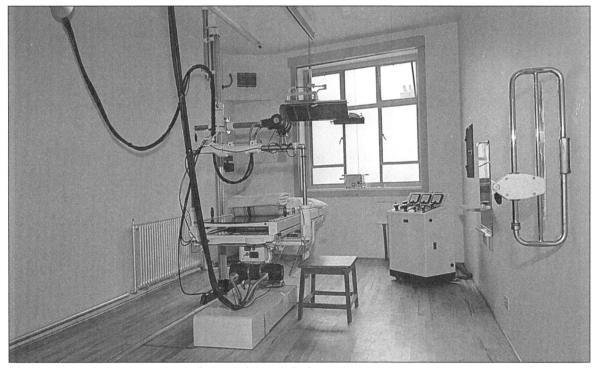

The new X-ray department at Newark General Hospital where £30,000 was spent on new extensions in 1958. (*110/Neg. 7203-5*)

The 20ft cabin cruiser, *Golden Age*, built by three employees of James Hole Brewery and named after the brewery's bottled light ale, is about to be launched in 1958. The three men involved in the project were Mr A.A. Stewart, Mr R. Morewood, and Mr R. Bennett. *(111/Neg. 7293)*

Military vehicles of the Sherwood Rangers Yeomanry in Newark Market Place during the Territorial Army golden jubilee service in 1958. *(112/Neg. 7296)*

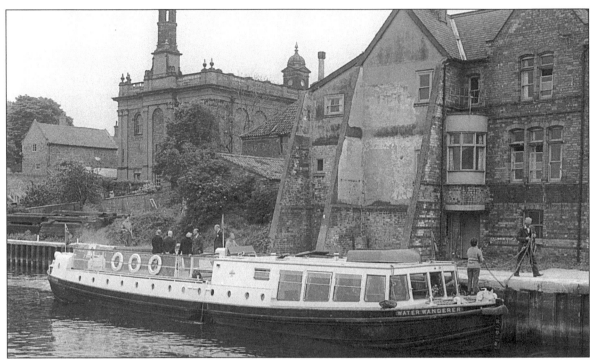

The *Water Wanderer*, British Waterways' luxury river cruiser, was launched in Newark in 1959 and went into passenger service cruising between Nottingham and Boston. *(113/Neg. 7765)*

July 1959 saw the worst ever traffic jams in Newark when roadworks on Trent Bridge caused eight-mile tailbacks along the Great North Road to Sutton-on-Trent. *(114/Neg. 7814)*

Hoses at the former
fire station on
Portland Street,
Newark, are cleaned
before being rolled
and put away in 1959.
(115/Neg. 7825)

The WVS was
presented a 'Meals on
Wheels' van by
Newark Round Table
in 1959. It was handed
over by the chairman
of the Round Table,
Mr Douglas Moutrie.
(116/Neg. 8035-2)

Royal Occasions

Princess Elizabeth visited RAF Cranwell in 1951 to inspect cadets. *(118/Neg. 1020-22)*

Princess Margaret attended Southwell Minster to celebrate 1,000 years of Christian worship in 1956. *(119/Neg. 4377)*

The Duchess of Kent reviewed aircraft instructors, students and ground crew on one of the runways at RAF Syerston. With her is station CO Group Capt. Gerald Warner DFC, AFC in 1960. *(120/Neg. 8484)*

The Duchess of Gloucester plants a tree in the grounds of Balderton Hospital during a visit in 1962. *(121/Neg. 10995-24)*

In 1963 The Duchess of Gloucester visited Southwell Minster for the 25th anniversary service of the North Midlands region of the WVS. She is pictured with the Provost of Southwell, the Very Revd Hugh Heywood, and the Lord Lieutenant of Nottinghamshire, Major-General Sir Robert Laycock. *(122/Neg. 11943)*

New entrant to the Jet Provost Flight Training Programme at RAF Cranwell in 1971 was Flight Lieutenant The Prince of Wales. *(123/Neg. 24874)*

A face in the crowd – off duty RAF Cranwell student Flight Lieutenant The Prince of Wales is just a face in the crowd watching an aerobatic display at RAF Cranwell in 1971. *(124/Neg. 25418)*

A proud day for the Duke of Edinburgh as he watches his son Prince Charles, receive his wings at RAF Cranwell's passing out parade. *(125/Neg. 25633-16)*

Prince Charles steps smartly away from the rostrum after receiving his wings. *(126/Neg. 25633-4)*

Princess Anne, with pupils of the Holy Trinity RC Primary School, Newark in 1971. *(127/Neg. 25006-30)*

Princess Anne also officially opened Southfield House, a block of elderly people's flats. One of the residents, Mrs Kate Whittington (left) is introduced by Mrs Douglas Blatherwick. *(128/Neg. 25006-34)*

Her Majesty The Queen visited RAF Cranwell in May 1975 to present a new Queen's Colour to the College. *(130/Neg. 32169)*

President of the East Midlands Tourist Board, Prince William of Gloucester, leaves Southwell Minster following an inspection of restoration work in 1971, escorted by Alderman Mrs Anne Yates, chairman of Notts County Council, and the Provost, The Very Revd Francis Pratt. *(129/Neg. 26244)*

After officially opening the new St Mark's Place shopping precinct in 1978, the Duchess of Kent visited Newark's historic market place, escorted by the Mayor of Newark, Councillor Roy Bird. *(131/Neg. 38581)*

Princess Margaret chats to four Brownies of the Swinderby Brownie Guide Pack and children of RAF Swinderby servicemen during a visit to the RAF station in 1976. *(132/Neg. 34473)*

Princess Alice, Dowager Duchess of Gloucester, visited RAF Swinderby in 1985 as Chief Commandant of the WRAF. *(133/Neg. 48680)*

Princess Anne, Colonel in Chief of the 3rd (Volunteer) Battalion of the Worcestershire and Sherwood Foresters Regiment presented their new colours in 1977. *(134/Neg. 35630-105)*

The Duchess of Gloucester pictured talking to staff at the official opening of Daloon Products UK Ltd, Newark in April 1984. *(135/Neg. 48905)*

Her Majesty The Queen and HRH The Duke of Edinburgh pose with Yeoman Warders outside the west door of Southwell Minster following the distribution of Maundy money. *(137/Neg. 48940-34)*

Members of Southwell clergy greet Her Majesty The Queen as she arrives at Southwell Minster for the Maundy Thursday service in 1984. *(136/Neg. 48940-65)*

The Sixties

The Queens Head Hotel provided a picturesque background when the South Notts Hunt met in Newark market place. *(138/Neg. 17108)*

The last 'get-together' for pupils and staff of Newark's Parish Church of England School in their Mount Lane playground before moving over to the Hercules Clay School in Barnby Road Newark in 1969. *(139/Neg. 21338-1)*

Dinner monitors at each table were introduced at the Mount School, Newark to eliminate queues at the serving hatch. *(140/Neg. 8836-3)*

Managing director of Worthington Simpson's Mr W.J.M. Adams bowls the first wood on the work's new bowls green. The bowls section of W-S Athletic Association was so well supported that in 1960 a second green was opened. *(142/Neg. 8323)*

This king-sized crane dominated the skyline of Newark during the construction of a new bottling plant at Holes Brewery near Beaumond Cross in 1960. *(141/Neg. 8172)*

In 1960 Sir Stuart Goodwin DL, JP visited the Newark unit of the Sea Cadet Corps and presented the unit with its proficiency certificate. Pictured receiving the certificate is Lt-Com. L. Hopesmith. *(143/Neg. 8429)*

South Collingham was in danger of losing one of its attractive rural scenes when fire severely damaged the thatched roof of a pair of cottages by the village green in 1960. *(144/Neg. 8532)*

The worst floods since 1947 affected Kelham Road, Newark. *(145/Neg. 8108-9)*

Dense fog and freezing weather caused difficulties for the police whilst ferrying food to water-bound Kelham Road residents. *(146/Neg. 8856-2)*

In dense fog this lorry owned by J.R. Marriott (Collingham) Ltd was struck by a diesel engine at South Muskham level crossing. *(147/Neg. 8740-2)*

Children near Caudwell's Mill, Southwell prepare to be splashed by vehicles passing through the flood waters. *(148/Neg. 8847-3)*

High winds tore a 60-foot cabin cruiser *Kitty Hawke* free from its moorings at Farndon Ferry. *(149/Neg. 8743)*

Three hundred members of the Notts Red Cross and friends attended an annual service and parade, held for the first time in Newark, at the Parish Church in 1960. *(150/Neg. 8288)*

In animated conversation are left to right, Mr and Mrs Holliwell, Dr Geoffrey Hine, Alderman Bernard Maule OBE JP, and Matron Miss E. Beamish in 1960 at the Newark General Hospital cocktail party held at the nurses' home on London Road. *(151/Neg. 8880)*

Top prizewinners at Newark Hospital's Assistant Nurse Training School are pictured with Mr R.P. Blatherwick JP who presented the awards at the school's first prizegiving in 1960. The assistant nurses were left to right, Mrs D.P. Bannerman, Miss B. North and Mrs G.D. Hunt. *(152/Neg. 8647-1)*

During the demolishing of Newark's courtroom in 1960, the old witness box was taken out. Pictured in the box is Mr William McCormack, foreman of the firm G.A. Pillatt and Son Ltd, builders of the new courthouse. *(153/Neg. 8687-2)*

Southwell Minister's tenor bell is lowered to floor level for re-casting, as part of a £5,000 tower alteration scheme in 1961. *(154/Neg. 8920)*

Watched by the Mayor of Newark, Alderman A.E. Whomsley, JP, and local Co-operative Society officials, the Mayoress makes the first purchases at the new supermarket, which opened, on Churchill Drive, Newark in 1961. *(155/Neg. 9180)*

The driver of this mini-car and his passengers, all strangers to Newark, found themselves in a tight spot in 1962 when they took a wrong turning out of Middlegate into Chain Lane, much to the surprise of pedestrians using the walkway. Notices at each end of the lane proclaim that cycling is prohibited… but there is no mention of cars. *(156/Neg. 10116)*

In 1962 a giant V-bomber crashed into a farmhouse in the tiny hamlet of Stubton killing two crew members and two residents. *(157/Neg. 10192)*

The pilot escaped unhurt when an American Air Force Super Sabre jet crashed near Cromwell in 1965. *(158/Neg. 14458)*

The two man crew of this wrecked Jet Provost trainer aircraft from RAF Syerston were killed when it crashed into a field at East Drayton near Newark in 1967. *(159/Neg. 17127)*

A fireman hoses down the roof and the remains of burnt-out cars in the destroyed showroom of the William Donald Ltd Garage on London Road, Newark in 1967. *(160/Neg. 18121)*

Knights Court, a group of old people's bungalows was opened in 1962 by Alderman J.H. Knight, JP. *(161/Neg. 10624)*

Members of Newark St John Ambulance Brigade in 1962. *(162/Neg. 10877)*

The opening of the Southwell RC Church in 1962. *(163/Neg. 10878)*

Her Majesty's inspector of constabulary Mr Sydney Lawrence chats with Sergeant A. Riley when he visited Newark Police Station in 1963. *(164/Neg. 12192)*

Grass-skirted ladies who attended Newark and District Flower Lovers Club Hawaiian dance night at Newark Town Hall in 1963. *(165/Neg. 12517)*

The biggest meal ever staged in Newark was held in a marquee on the site of the new Cardinal Hinsley School on Grange Road in 1963. The 'loyalty dinner' was attended by 620 people. The dinner was held to raise funds to meet the cost of building two new schools. *(166/Neg. 12583)*

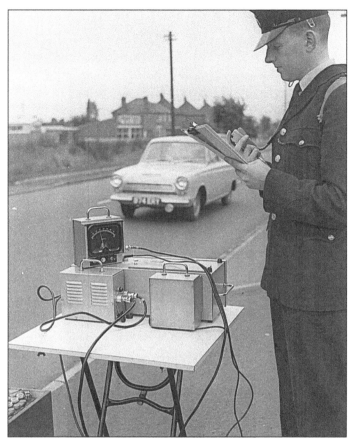

Assistant Bishop of Southwell, the Right Revd Mark Way, with the Revd Eric J. Kingsnorth who was instituted as vicar of Newark in 1963. *(168/Neg. 12407-2)*

In 1963 Newark Police demonstrated new vehicle speed checking equipment. *(167/Neg. 12368)*

This van plunged 15 feet down the embankment on to the partially constructed Newark by-pass in 1963. *(169/Neg. 12735)*

In 1963 Fireman William Anderson directs a jet of water in the upper floor of the burning building of Tournay and Sons Ltd, the decorators in Baldertongate, Newark. *(170/Neg. 12776)*

Fire gutted the premises of Gilstrap Earp and Co, on Northgate, Newark in 1964 causing an estimated £50,000 of damage. *(171/Neg. 13054)*

Fire at the Benefit footwear shop in Newark Market Place during 1965 caused severe disruption and thousands of pounds of damage; as a precaution the nearby Clinton Arms Hotel was evacuated. *(172/Neg. 14641)*

Firemen fight a blaze at Associated British Maltsters warehouse on Northgate, Newark, in 1969. *(173/Neg. 21560)*

Concrete beams destined for the A1 by-pass construction site, created an unusual bridge, when traffic was directed beneath them to avoid congestion in 1964. (*174/Neg. 13102*)

An increase in traffic in Newark town centre in 1964, necessitated the demolition of two cottages to make way for a car park in Appletongate Newark. (*175/Neg. 13988*)

Newark's ancient Market Place cobbles were re-laid in 1965. *(176/Neg. 14718-11)*

The market stalls were found a temporary site on the Lombard street car park, whilst the re-laying of the cobbles was carried out. *(177/Neg. 14719)*

The famous steam engine, *The Flying Scotsman*, passed through Northgate station at more than 70mph during a 500-mile round trip from Darlington to King's Cross London and back in 1965. *(178/Neg. 14634-7)*

Newark's civic leaders process to the Parish church for a memorial service for former Prime Minister Sir Winston Churchill in 1965. *(179/Neg. 14355)*

Shades of *Dr Who.* A life-size dalek made by a parent, was one of the attractions at the Newark Preparatory School's annual fete in 1965. *(180/Neg. 14847-5)*

Steeplejacks near the top of the 240-foot Parish Church spire, to examine the 146-year-old weathervane, in the shape of a cockerel which had its tail partly blasted away during a storm in 1965. *(181/Neg. 15183-11)*

The newly-repaired and re-gilded weathervane before being put back on top of the church spire in 1965. *(182/Neg. 15564-9)*

In 1969 Newark Cricket Club's ground on Kelham Road became the new home for a score box that had previously been used at Lord's, the headquarters of English cricket. *(183/Neg. 21399)*

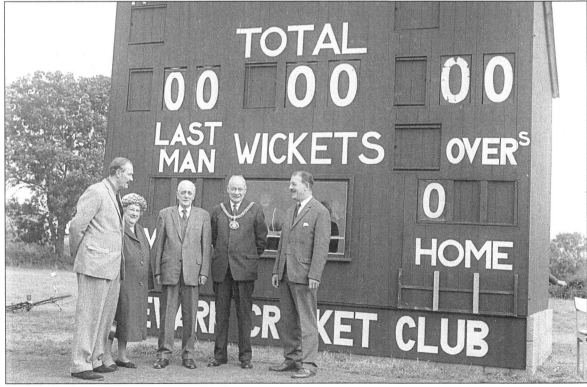

The county match between Lancashire and Nottinghamshire in 1966 is viewed from the score box at Elm Avenue Sports Ground in Newark. *(184/Neg. 16420)*

County cricket at the Ransome and Marles Sports Ground on Elm Avenue, Newark, attracted a large crowd to watch Nottinghamshire play Leicestershire in 1967. *(185/Neg. 18017-6)*

Firemen sift through the remains of a burnt out caravan – home to a young family in Glovers Lane, Balderton in 1967. *(186/Neg. 17351)*

Severe gales blew down this 60 foot Wych Elm tree, which blocked Low Street, Collingham to traffic for six hours in 1967. *(187/Neg. 17366)*

Anglican member of Christ Church Newark, Dr Sidney Radley lays a foundation stone at Hawtonville's new Methodist Church in 1967. *(188/Neg. 17939-4)*

Eight-year-old Jonathan Whiles of Valley Prospect, Newark places a jar containing a penny under the foundation stone, to represent the saving of pennies in jam-jars, by church members, to raise the funds to build the new church. *(189/Neg. 17939-3)*

Demolition of farm buildings at Balderton in 1967 resulted in the unexpected, when they fell on the nearby Methodist Church Hall knocking down this four-year-old building. *(190/Neg. 18000)*

Grandfather time was moved to Sweden, when Newark antiques dealer, Mr Geoffrey Whittaker, exported these clocks in 1967. *(191/Neg. 18567)*

Staff from Newark hotels and restaurants took part in the 6th annual pancake races in Newark Market Place to raise money for charity in 1968. *(192/Neg. 18773)*

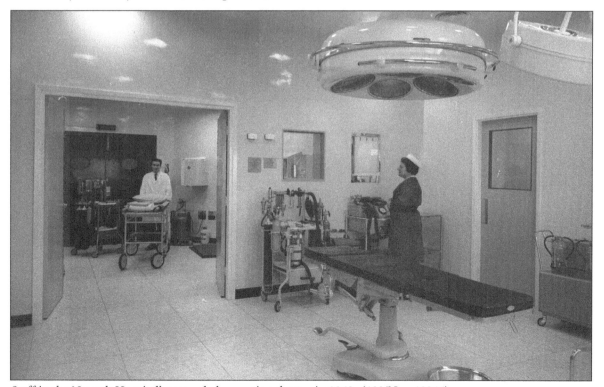

Staff in the Newark Hospital's upgraded operating theatre in 1968. *(193/Neg. 19246)*

Pictured in her mini skirt measuring 13in from waistband to hem, 24-year-old Mrs Sylvia Feeney of 48 Marsh Lane, Farndon won a 'miniest miniskirt' competition held at The Willow Tree Inn, Barnby-in-the-Willows in 1968. *(194/Neg. 19399)*

A large crowd at Southwell Show watches the tug of war contest in 1968. *(195/Neg. 19559)*

The villain in the stocks at Newark Traders Association's Medieval Market in 1968. *(196/Neg. 19750-10)*

In 1968 the *Newark Advertiser*'s new Solna web offset press from Sweden was the first to be installed by any newspaper in the country. *(197/Neg. 21139)*

Ransome and Marles band pictured in the factory's canteen while recording a concert in 1969 for BBC Radio 4. (*198/Neg. 20246-1*)

Lineout action during a match between Newark Rugby Club and a touring team of Dutch Navy Cadets, in 1969. (*199/Neg. 20699*)

Pictured at work at Staythorpe is railman Mr Alfred Shelton of South Muskham celebrated 45 years' service with British Rail in 1969. *(200/Neg. 20774)*

Reluctant to take part in the grand parade of cattle during the 1969 Newark agricultural show, this Hereford bull went on a rampage across the showground with two herdsmen in tow. *(201/Neg. 20811-135)*

Newark Regatta held at Winthorpe provided this sparkling picture as the sun reflected on the water as one of the 'eights' was about to pass under the Newark by-pass bridge in 1969. *(202/Neg. 20912)*

Collingham Ladies Football Team pictured in 1969. *(203/Neg. 20975)*

In 1969 sixth formers of Magnus Grammar School give a cheer for senior history master, Councillor Leslie Carswell, after hearing he is to be the Mayor of Newark. *(204/Neg. 20590)*

A spectacular production of *The Yeomen of the Guard* was staged at Newark Castle grounds in 1969. *(205/Neg. 21103)*

Newark firemen practising in the drill yard of the new £80,000 Fire Station in Boundary Road, Newark, which opened in 1969. *(206/Neg. 21187)*

Panda cars were introduced to Newark in 1969 as part of a new unit beat policing system. *(207/Neg. 21723)*

Mr Roy Wells spent 30 years acquiring one of the largest private collections of folk history in Britain which was exhibited in a warehouse in Portland Street, Newark in 1969. *(208/Neg. 21840-1)*

One of the most colourful live shows ever presented in Newark was *The Merry Widow*, a musical comedy performed by Newark Operatic Society at the Palace Theatre in 1960. Principals in the centre of the picture were Wendy Smith playing the wealthy widow, Anna Glavari, and Peter Hughes-Williams (Count Danio). *(209/Neg. 8211)*

Iain McKenzie, assistant brewer with James Hole and Co in Newark is checking his beer stocks ready for the festive season in December 1969. *(210/Neg. 21989)*

Scenes and Changing
Face of the District

The historic town of Newark on Trent pictured in 1964 providing aerial views of the slighted castle, and the church of St Mary Magdalene. *(211/Neg. 31478-10)*

The scene through the window of Newark Castle has always had the River Trent to form a constant foreground from the changing skyline. *(213/Neg. 29264)*

A barge passes Newark Castle and a now demolished riverside building in 1952. *(212/Neg. 1417-1)*

The town wharf in the 1970s before the regeneration of the riverside. *(215/Neg. 23279-6)*

Collingham Row in 1955. These houses were regarded unfit for habitation and were marked for slum clearance having no indoor piped water and just a communal back yard. *(216/Neg. 4087)*

In 1959 these tiny cottages in Lilley's Row, Newark, which were completely devoid of bathrooms and modern sanitation, were pulled down as part of Newark's slum clearance programme. *(217/Neg. 7800-2)*

Scales Row, a dingy huddle of weavers' cottages in Farndon Road, Newark, were demolished as part of the slum clearance drive in 1959. These cottages were home to generations of Newarkers who wove the linen for which the town was once famed. *(218/Neg. 7520-2)*

A petition sent to Newark Corporation by Mrs Terence Player (left) and Mrs Nigel Newstead (right) in 1972 resulted in a line of cottages in Union Row, off King Street, Newark, being demolished as they were unsuitable for habitation. *(219/Neg. 27904)*

In 1956 the Lloyds Bank on the corner of Stodman Street and Castlegate was demolished to make way for a modern building. *(220/Neg. 4589-2)*

The new Lloyds Bank in 1958. *(221/Neg. 7365)*

The 14th century Beaumond Cross monument pictured on its former site at the junction of the A46, the Old Great North Road and Cartergate in 1950. *(222/Neg. 467)*

A new home for Beaumond Cross which was moved to London Road Gardens in November 1974. The cross, which dates back to 1300, was re-sited a second time. It was last moved a few yards in the early 1900s. *(223/Neg. 31182)*

In 1957 the Fosseway at Bargate in Newark was always congested with traffic. This narrow bottleneck was widened with the loss of several landmarks including Houlton's the bakers, Porters the butchers, Miss Wright's confectionery and Hopkinson's the saddlers. *(224/Neg. 6046)*

The ancient tithe barn in Lover's Lane, Newark in 1958 before the whole area was victim of slum clearance. *(225/Neg. 7393)*

The site between Northgate and Lover's Lane where for centuries Newark's tithe barn stood, now presents a different picture as building work proceeds and new blocks of flats begin to take shape. *(226/Neg. 8533-3)*

The completed flats in the redeveloped area of Newark. *(227/Neg. 8890-1)*

A view of Newark Parish Church which had been hidden for generations was revealed in 1960 when workmen completed the demolition of a block of cottages and shops on the London Road side of Baldertongate, the first stage of a road-widening scheme. *(228/Neg. 8434-1)*

Demolition of the gas works on Barnbygate, Newark to make room for a new Curry's warehouse in 1960. *(229/Neg. 8482-2)*

Pictured in 1970 – 110ft across by 20ft deep this hole used to contain a gasometer for Newark's old gasworks built in 1902. It is to form the basement of a new warehouse for Curry's Electrical Stores. *(230/Neg. 23021)*

Construction of the five-storey blocks of flats in Northgate, the highest dwellings in the district, changing Newark's skyline in 1961. *(231/Neg. 9755)*

Pictured in 1967 are the Mayor of Newark, Councillor Joseph Beaumont, left, and Alan Burt, PR officer for developers George Wimpey and Co, looking at the newly-completed Fosseway estate, which marks the end of the Newark Corporation's post-war housing estate programme. Since World War Two some 2,800 council homes have been built in Newark. *(232/Neg. 18232)*

The modern St Leonard's Church and Bridge Community Centre, Lincoln Road, Newark was officially opened in 1978. *(233/Neg. 38088)*

Demolition of the old St Leonard's Church, Lover's Lane, Newark. *(234/Neg. 38924)*

A new look to the horizon in the Boundary Road area of Newark as the new Roman Catholic Church's slim-line spire was erected in 1976. *(235/Neg. 34291)*

Newark's new bus station on Lombard Street in 1964. *(236/Neg. 14100)*

The St Mark's Lane shopping precinct, Newark started to take shape in November 1976. *(237/Neg. 34787)*

A view of the St Mark's Lane development in August 1977 as seen from the Parish Church tower. *(238/Neg. 36153)*

Newark's elegant Town Hall built between 1774 and 1776 overlooks the market place in the town centre. *(239/Neg. 27502)*

In the late 1980s Newark Town Hall, one of the finest Georgian town halls in England, was restored to its former glory. Pictured is the Adam style ballroom with its ornate ceiling. *(240/Neg. 64753)*

The Moot Hall in Newark Market Place, former seat of local government in Newark before the building of the present Town Hall in 1773, pictured in 1964 prior to extensive preservation work. *(241/Neg. 14124)*

The refurbished Moot Hall pictured in 1967 and occupied by an electrical retailer's shop. *(242/Neg. 18268)*

Newark has many narrow courtyards and alleyways often missed by visitors to the town. One of these, Chain Lane (above) is a busy shopping thoroughfare from the market place to Middlegate. *(243/Neg. 23164-1)*

The Savoy Cinema in Middlegate, Newark pictured in 1965 has now been converted to building society premises. *(244/Neg. 15282-6)*

Crowds line a bridge on the new A1 bypass to watch as the first official car passes along the dual carriageway in 1964. *(245/Neg. 13700)*

Pictured in 1969, the curving old A1 divides the houses of Grove Street, Balderton from the newly-constructed sports centre and the Grove Comprehensive School. *(246/Neg. 3478-87)*

The dedication of Collingham's village cross by the Vicar, Canon Rupert Stevens. The cross stood on the east side of High Street for about 600 years but in 1972 was relocated across the road where the Parish Council were developing a public open space. *(247/Neg. 27876)*

The often-filmed gates and façade of the RAF College Cranwell pictured in 1971. *(249/Neg. 24874-A)*

An open day at Kelham Hall's Theological College in 1969 enabled visitors to view the splendour of the College Chapel. *(251/Neg. 21263)*

An aerial view of the village of Kelham (three miles from Newark). On the right the bridge spans the River Trent, with Kelham Hall (centre) and the church (left). *(250/Neg.67116-31)*

The town of Southwell dominated by the magnificent cathedral church which was built on the site of a Saxon Minster founded in 956 AD. *(252/Neg. 67116-34)*

Personalities

Professor Harold Laski whose Newark market place speech during the 1945 General Election gave rise to the Laski libel action. In his speech Professor Laski advocated revolution by violence to achieve reform. The *Newark Advertiser* reported what was said. *(253)*

Lord Goddard, the Lord Chief Justice in 1946, who presided over the Laski case in the High Court. The trial in November and December lasted five days and was heard before a special jury. *(254)*

Mr Cyril Parlby, editor of the *Newark Advertiser* at the time of the Laski case. He was named as defendant with the newspaper. The jury found for the defence and Laski had to pay £15,000 costs, a big sum in 1946. The newspaper's justification plea was upheld. *(255/Neg.34015)*

Richard Dimbleby recording an interview for the *Down Your Way* radio programme with Mrs Joan McLeish, a worker at Newark Egg Packers in 1951. *(256/Neg. 787)*

Raymond Mays, the famous motorist, is seen having his car filled with petrol at the Castlegate garage of Brooks Motor Company (Newark) Ltd in 1953. *(257/Neg. 1742)*

Treasurer of the Labour Party, the Right Hon. Hugh Gaitskell, addressed the third annual dinner of the Newark Labour Party in 1955. He is shown on the left with Mr George Deer, OBE, MP (centre) and Councillor P.M. Carmody (secretary of the Newark Labour Party). *(258/Neg. 4069)*

At a celebration dinner at Newark Town Hall in 1957 Earl Attlee presented Newark's MP Mr George Deer with a gold watch to mark Mr Deer's 50 years membership of the Labour Party. *(259/Neg. 6082-1)*

The Right Hon. Harold Wilson, Shadow Chancellor of the Exchequer (second from left), was the guest of honour at Newark Labour Party's dinner held at the Town Hall in November 1958. *(260/Neg. 7424)*

Politician Enoch Powell holds two wine glasses aloft as he speaks to Newark Conservatives in 1969. *(262/Neg. 20732-22)*

Harold Macmillan addresses a large crowd in 1959 in Newark Market Place. *(261/Neg. 7930-1)*

Labour Party Deputy Leader George Brown speaking at an open air meeting in Newark market place to commemorate the 50th anniversary of Newark Labour Party in 1969. *(263/Neg. 21598)*

Mr Robert Wilkinson, Newark Conservative Party chairman (right), assisted the Secretary of State for Foreign and Commonwealth Affairs, Sir Alec Douglas Home, with the tape cutting during the opening of Newark Conservatives new offices and club, Belvedere, London Road, Newark in 1972. *(264/Neg. 27325)*

Prime Minister Edward Heath visited Winthorpe Show Ground in July 1973 and is pictured with a wry smile on his face as he watches the South Notts Pony Club in training. *(265/Neg. 29154-27)*

Secretary of State for Northern Ireland, the Right Hon. William Whitelaw, visited Holy Trinity Church Hall, Newark in 1973. *(266/Neg. 29591)*

Leader of the opposition, Mrs Margaret Thatcher, chatting to shoppers in Newark market place during a visit to the town in 1977. *(267/Neg. 35345)*

The wartime exploits of Newark's Lt-Col. Sam Derry DSO, MC, TD, JP in German occupied Rome, where he organised an escape line for 4,000 allied prisoners, were published as a book called the *Rome Escape Line*. The story was first published in shortened form as a series of articles in the *Newark Advertiser*, when the writer was *Advertiser* chief reporter Peter Lord (right). *(268/Neg. 8478-3)*

In 1983 Lt-Col. Sam Derry (right) had a surprise reunion with Father Sean Quinlan who assisted him in his wartime escapades in Rome during World War Two. *(269/Neg. 47977)*

Lt-Col. Basil Ringrose, pictured with a gold and silver cigarette case bearing the royal coat of arms from Emperor Haile Selassie of Ethopia, was honoured for the part he played in liberating the country during World War Two. In 1941 he commanded 20,000 Ethiopians to harry the south flank of the occupying Italian forces. *(270/Neg. 16224)*

Wartime memories were revived again when Group Captain Leonard Cheshire VC (left) chats with Squadron Leader Johnny Johnson of Collingham when they met at the opening of welfare homes in Farndon. Both men served with the famous 617 Squadron when it was stationed at RAF Scampton. Group Captain Cheshire took over command of the squadron after Guy Gibson was killed. *(272/Neg. 28922)*

Rear-Admiral Robert Sherbrooke greets the Queen in 1968 in his capacity as Lord Lieutenant of Nottinghamshire. *(271/Neg. 19088)*

The Archbishop of Canterbury, the Most Revd and Right Hon. Arthur Michael Ramsey (left) is given a cheer by the students as he throws his 'Canterbury cap' into the air. He was leaving Kelham Hall after visiting the Society of the Sacred Mission in 1963. *(273/Neg. 11676)*

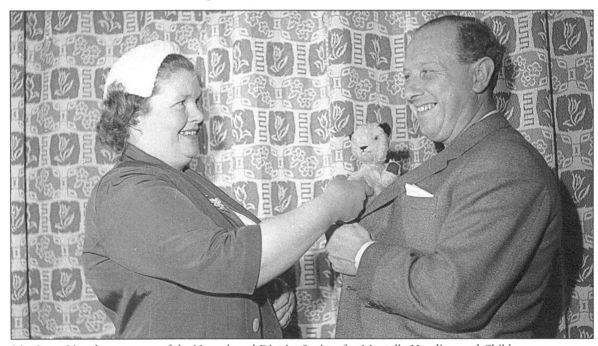

Mrs Joyce Lincoln, secretary of the Newark and District Society for Mentally Handicapped Children, was introduced to Harry Corbett and Sooty, the famous TV teddy bear, at a cocktail party in aid of the society in 1960. *(274/Neg. 8281-2)*

Comedian Ken Dodd was in Newark to open a solid fuel central heating show house in the Parklands Estate, Hawton Road in 1964. *(275/Neg. 14105)*

Actress Pat Phoenix otherwise known as Elsie Tanner from *Coronation Street* visited residents at Knight's Court, Newark in 1968. *(276/Neg. 19796)*

Norman Wisdom visited Balderton Hospital in 1974 to present a Sunshine Coach on behalf of the Variety Club of Great Britain. *(277/Neg. 30872)*

Jimmy Savile visited the Grove Comprehensive School, Balderton in 1976. *(278/Neg. 34624)*

TV personality Lady Isobel Barnett (left) was the chief guest at Balderton Women's Institute's 25th anniversary dinner at Newark Town Hall in 1971. She is pictured with the Institute's president, Mrs Rose Pratt. *(279/Neg. 25060)*

Disc Jockey Jimmy Young was carried away by three contestants in a Miss Hot Pants competition at Newark Rugby Club's carnival in 1971. *(280/Neg. 25372)*

Peter Adamson, better known as Len Fairclough of *Coronation Street*, with contestants in the Miss Hot Pants contest at Newark Rugby Club Carnival in 1972. *(281/Neg. 27236)*

Stars of TV's *Emmerdale Farm*, Stan Richards (Seth Armstrong), and Richard Thorp (Alan Turner), took an interest in the prize-winning cattle when they visited Notts County Agricultural Show at Newark Showground in 1988. *(282/Neg. 58125-8)*

TV personality, Noele Gordon of *Crossroads* fame, opened Balderton Hospital's hydrotherapy pool in 1978. (*283/Neg. 36848*)

After opening Balderton Hospital's annual show, famous disc jockey Pete Murray couldn't resist visiting the show discotheque to put a record on the turntable in 1967. (*284/Neg. 18032*)

The famous Beatles pop group, George, Ringo, John and Paul, unexpectedly turned up at the Old England Hotel, Sutton-on-Trent for a meal. They were on their way from London to Bradford in 1964. *(285/Neg. 13962)*

Cliff Richard who was appearing at Newark's Palace Theatre in January 1959 was presented with a doll of himself by Newark's well-known doll collector, Mrs Vina Cooke. *(286/Neg. 7560)*

Englebert Humperdinck visited Newark briefly in 1967 and took the opportunity to tour Newark Castle. *(287/Neg. 17553)*

Lonnie Donegan is pictured signing one of his LP sleeves, while enjoying a cup of tea in the Savoy Café, Newark, in 1962. He is pictured with Miss M. Golland, manageress of the Savoy Café and cashier Mrs P. Wilson. *(288/Neg. 11247)*

Celebrated jazz trumpeter Kenny Ball was at Balderton's Grove Sports Centre in 1971 for the Newark Police Ball. *(289/Neg. 25085)*

Service with a smile from singer/comedian Roy Castle when he entertained from behind the bar during his visit for lunch at the Plough Inn, Coddington in 1972. *(290/Neg. 27830)*

Society photographer, Lord Lichfield and arch Goon, Sir Harry Secombe, were the two star guests at a Caribbean ball held at Kelham Hall in 1981 in aid of Dr Barnardo's. *(291/Neg. 44084-12)*

Southwell was the last stop on a 45-minute chase around Nottinghamshire for Anneka Rice and her flying TV crew, when they were searching for clues for the Channel 4 programme, *Treasure Hunt*, in 1985. *(292/Neg. 51553-32)*

Actor David Kossoff takes his text from the Bible for his one-man performance at Southwell Minster in October 1973. *(293/Neg. 29579)*

Violin virtuoso, Yehudi Menhuin, officially opened the Newark School of Violin Making by playing unaccompanied Bach. The Violin School is housed in the former premises of The National Westminster Bank Limited on Kirkgate, Newark. *(294/Neg. 37286)*

Miss World, Lesley Langley, at the opening ceremony of the East Midlands Caravan Exhibition at Farndon Road, Newark in 1966. *(295/Neg. 16724)*

Miss World Madeleine Hartog Bel, pictured with Station Inspector Albert Warner and some young admirers, when she called at Northgate railway station, whilst en route from London to Lincoln in 1967. *(296/Neg. 18486)*

In 1967 Balderton-born Shakespearian actor Sir Donald Wolfit and Lady Wolfit joined the audience at the Robin Hood Theatre Averham in October to watch a performance of Sheridan's *The Rivals*. Earlier in the year Sir Donald had bought the theatre and vested it in the custody of trustees. *(297/Neg. 18306)*

Harry Wheatcroft, the famous rose grower, presented Mayor of Newark Alderman Mrs Elizabeth Yorke with a bouquet of his blooms when he visited Newark Town Hall in 1973. *(298/Neg. 29505)*

Something amusing caught the attention of Dr and Mrs Denys Hine of Newark and Mr John Eastwood (left) of Oxton Manor when they were pictured at a ball in aid of Cancer Research at Mr Eastwood's home in 1973. *(299/Neg. 29023)*

Ted Bishop, MP for Newark, and Minister of State for Agriculture (centre), chats with two Newark Mayors – Mayor of Newark, New Jersey, Mr Kenneth Gibson (right) and Mayor of Newark-on-Trent, Councillor Roy Bird, pictured at a civic reception to greet Mr Gibson during his visit in 1978. *(300/Neg. 38511)*

England and Kent wicketkeeper Alan Knott in typical pose, when Kent played Nottinghamshire in a county cricket match at Elm Avenue sports ground, Newark in 1969. *(301/Neg. 21054-7)*

Derek Underwood, Kent and England bowler signs autographs during the match between Notts and Kent. *(302/Neg. 21054-8)*

Tony Lock, Leicestershire and former Surrey and England spin bowler, watches his team batting against Nottinghamshire in the county cricket match held at Elm Avenue Sports Ground, Newark in 1967. *(303/Neg. 18017-5)*

Fans mob Notts skipper Gary Sobers after he scored a century against Worcestershire in a Sunday League match at the Elm Avenue Sports Ground, Newark in August 1971. *(304/Neg. 25579)*

England's heavyweight boxer Joe Bugner pictured signing autographs for fans when he lunched at the Saracen's Head Hotel, Southwell in 1970. *(305/Neg. 23115)*

Tommy Lawton, the then manager of Notts County FC, is presenting the Robert Burden Cup to Bottesford Youth 'A' captain Ray Levesley after his team had won the cup, beating Balderton Old Boys Juniors by three goals to nil in 1958. *(306/Neg. 7169)*

Nottingham Forest footballer Bobby McKinlay and Newark hospital matron Miss E. Jordan push over a pile of 10,500 pennies, collected for hospital funds, on the bar at the French Horn public house, Upton in 1969. *(307/Neg. 20799)*

Sir Stanley Matthews signs his autograph for ten-year-old Harold Heeley at a celebrity football match organised by Newark Round Table in 1970. *(308/Neg. 22239-B)*

In 1978 Nottingham Forest Supporters' Club chairman, Mr Dave Crocker, presented Brian Clough with a gavel when the Forest manager visited the Robin Hood Hotel, Newark to speak to Forest supporters. *(309/Neg. 36888)*

The Seventies

More than 300 years after the end of the Civil War, Newark was again the scene for several sieges. Newark Castle, 'slighted' by the Parliamentarians after the 17th-century hostilities, provided a magnificent backdrop in 1972 for the re-enactment by the Cavaliers and Roundheads of one of the Civil War battles. *(310/Neg. 27651)*

Fashion models clad in bikinis and sheltering under umbrellas, strolled around the Newark and Nottingham-shire Agricultural Show in 1971 well prepared for the sunshine and showers which were forecast for the event. *(311/Neg. 14139)*

Bikinis were also appropriate for this 'Isle of Capri' float, one of the entries in Southwell's carnival parade in the early 1970s. *(312/Neg. 22920)*

A facing both ways Mini with owner Mr Malcolm Streets in the background. On the left is Frank Jessop and at the wheel on the right Mr Neville Holmes. The car was built from two wrecked Mini vans at Mr Jessop's Collingham garage during 1970 and was capable of being driven in both directions. *(313/Neg. 22992)*

Vicar of Newark the Revd Ben Lewers was one of the subjects interviewed by Brian Johnston for Radio 4's *Down Your Way* programme in 1978. *(314/Neg. 38610)*

In 1970 the River Trent at Newark was drained so that the foundations of the bridges could be examined. *(315/Neg. 23241)*

In 1970 Walter Winterbottom, director of the Sports Council, opened the £200,000 Grove Sports Centre, Balderton. He is pictured wielding a foil with Mrs Hilda Bilton, chairman of Newark Rural District Council, and Councillor Alaric Hine, who was chairman of the Grove Sports Centre joint management committee. *(316/Neg. 22223)*

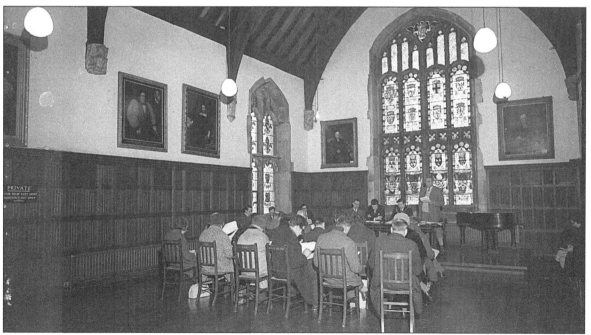

Members of Southwell Rural District Council met in the grandeur of the Great Hall, Bishop's Manor. They were using the premises instead of the council chamber as it was being redecorated. *(317/Neg. 22232)*

Members of Ransome Hoffmann Pollard Works Band in 1970. *(318/Neg. 22315)*

Gail Hudson is welcomed back from America with her heart defects cured thanks to a long fund-raising campaign by the *Newark Advertiser* and donations from its readers. *(319/Neg. 22430)*

Francesca Dixon (21) won the title of Miss Collingham in 1970. Francesca lived at The White House, Low Street, Collingham and worked at the Singer Sewing Machine Company in Newark. *(320/Neg. 22244)*

Dennis Linsey of Cherry Holt is pictured with a 20lb 4oz pike which he caught at the Railway Pond, Balderton in 1970. *(321/Neg. 22273)*

Local artist, Sam Burden, made this snow sculpture of the Venus de Milo in his garden in Bancroft Road, Newark in March 1970. *(322/Neg. 22274)*

'Let's Go Walkabout' in Newark Market Place – an experimental pedestrianisation scheme commenced in 1970. *(323/Neg. 22454)*

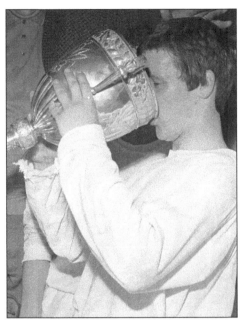

Pictured in 1970 the procession of clergy into Southwell Minster for the installation of the new provost, the Very Revd Francis Pratt (third from the left). *(324/Neg. 22505)*

A. Cooling, captain of Worthington Simpson Football Club, who defeated Notts Combined Police in the Notts Alliance Senior Knock-Out Cup Final in 1970, takes a celebratory swig from the cup. *(325/Neg. 22529-1)*

The victorious Worthington Simpson football team. *(326/Neg. 22529-2)*

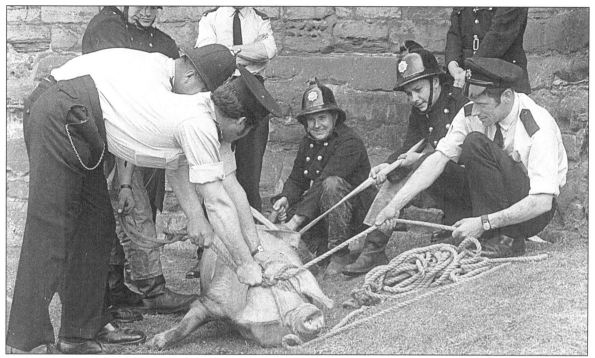

Police and firemen combined to calm down a tethered sow after her dip in the River Trent following a dash from Newark Cattle Market. *(327/Neg. 22586)*

In 1970 the band and drums of the 1st Battalion of the Worcestershire and Sherwood Foresters Regiment led by the regimental mascot, ram Derby XXI, marched through Newark for the first time. The salute was taken by the Mayor and Mayoress of Newark, Councillor and Mrs Richard Lamb. *(328/Neg. 23170)*

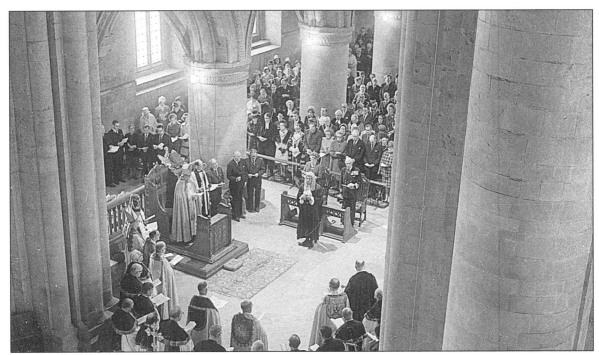

Bishops, members of the chapter, and other church dignitaries surround the bishop's throne during the enthronement of the new Bishop of Southwell, the Right Revd Denis Wakeling, at Southwell Minster in 1970. *(329/Neg. 23259)*

During a Georgian market organised by the Newark Tradesmen's Association in 1973 Superintendent Minister of the Newark Methodist Circuit, the Revd Eric Roe, re-enacted John Wesley's trip to Newark Market Place. *(330/Neg. 29352)*

Reflecting bygone years – unusual and antique items on display at Collingham Memorial Hall in 1973, were reflected in one of the exhibits. *(332/Neg. 29418)*

Newark's town treasures, valued at £500,000 in 1974, went on view to the public in the Town Hall. *(331/Neg. 29835-8)*

In 1971 Mrs Beatrice Richardson (75), a resident of Howes Court, Newark congratulates Alderman Thomas Howes who opened the flats named after him. *(333/Neg. 25199)*

Members of the 11th Newark Battalion of the Notts Home Guard were on duty again to take advantage of a free offer from Newark's Savoy Cinema manager, Mr Ronald Marsh (left). Old comrades reunited in 1971 after 26 years to watch the comedy film *Dad's Army*. *(334/Neg. 25148)*

Lady footballers pose for the camera at the Queen's Silver Jubilee celebrations at Greenway, Newark in 1977. *(335/Neg. 35812)*

Children of Nursery Avenue, Farndon pictured at their Jubilee Party. *(336/Neg. 35790)*

Mr William Fox of Windsor Road, Newark pictured in 1971 in his garden with his 70-year-old telescope which he used to study Jupiter. *(337/Neg. 25476)*

In October 1971 Mr Roland Hoggard of Prior Farm, Thurgarton faced a stiff task in putting back the time on the 80 clocks scattered around his home. *(338/Neg. 25978)*

Newark's first traffic warden, Mr Philip James Price, took the to the streets in July 1972. *(340/Neg. 27387)*

The Middlegate broom brigade made a clean sweep and won the title of Newark's Tidiest Street. The contest was run in 1972 as part of the first 'Keep Newark Tidy' week. *(339/Neg. 27598)*

Humber Navigator, the biggest barge to reach Newark from Hull since 1952, docks outside Major and Co Ltd's Northgate premises in 1975. *(342/Neg. 32806-1)*

Despite being landed a two-footed drop kick by Tony Cortez of London, at the Grove Sports Centre, Balderton in 1971, Pete Smith of Newark won the British lightweight title. *(341/Neg. 24664)*

About 1,800 employees of Ransome Hoffman and Pollard Ltd gathered in the car park in 1972 to vote during industrial action. *(343/Neg. 27091)*

In 1972 militant postman, Mr Andrew Boggie, made national TV news when he squatted in a tree for several weeks in a desperate attempt to save an ancient elm which Newark Town Council had been advised had to be felled. *(344/Neg. 27432)*

Ministry officials disinfect their boots before entering a farm on Tolney Lane, Newark in February 1973 during the outbreak of swine vesicular disease. *(345/Neg. 28408)*

Housewives queue for the 'Staff of Life' outside L. Day and Sons, bakery on Bridge Street, Newark when bread workers went on strike in December 1974. *(346/Neg. 31274)*

Tragedy struck in September 1975 when 10 'weekend' soldiers on an army exercise died. Their boat went over the weir at Cromwell Lock. An RAF rescue helicopter hovers inches over the water whilst a winch man searches for the bodies of the dead soldiers. *(347/Neg. 32753)*

Fire gutted the last Avro Anson Mk XI in the world at the Newark (Notts and Lincs) Air Museum at Winthorpe Airfield in 1971. *(348/Neg. 25150)*

In 1970 a fire at Reg Day and Co Ltd, Newark which caused an estimated £30,000 worth of damage. *(349/Neg. 22133)*

The dramatic scene in Newark's Victoria Street in 1973 when workers formed a human chain to salvage stock as firemen doused the blaze at Cooper and Co clothing company. *(350/Neg. 29314)*

Fire gutted Queensway Furniture Warehouse in Appletongate, Newark in December 1973 causing an estimated £250,000 damage. *(351/Neg. 29725)*

Fire destroyed the disused maltings on Farndon Road, Newark in August 1975. *(353/Neg. 32541)*

Homes on Winthorpe Road housing estate were evacuated when fire destroyed the lacquer department of Croda Polymers Ltd in Newark in 1974. *(352/Neg. 30863)*

Fire roared through the coffee bar in Kirkgate Newark in January 1977. *(354/Neg. 35033)*

A gas explosion rocked Queens Court, Newark, wrecking two District Council maisonettes in January 1977. *(355/Neg. 35087)*

Firemen fight a fire at the warehouse of the Clarks of Newark in George Street in 1977. *(356/Neg. 36041)*

The final scene, with the lights of the 30ft pagoda shining against the silhouette of the castle wall, during a performance of the *Mikado* in 1971. *(357/Neg. 25389-35)*

Slave auctioneer John Coles sells his wares in Newark Market Place during the Oriental Market in 1971. The slave was 25-year-old Shirley White of Collingham who was sold for a bargain price of £2. *(358/Neg. 25453-3)*

173

Youngsters at Work and Play

Young pupils learn counting skills at Balderton's newly-opened Chuter Ede primary school in 1967. *(359/Neg. 17306)*

A classroom scene at the new Bishop Alexander School, Newark, which opened in January 1955. *(360/Neg. 2828)*

New-style classrooms at Southwell's Lowes Wong Infant School which opened in January 1971. *(361/Neg. 24596)*

The Roman Catholic Bishop of Nottingham, the Right Revd Edward Ellis, gives children his blessing as he enters the Holy Trinity RC school for its official opening in 1971. *(362/Neg. 25429)*

Youngsters gather around the high diving boards at the opening of the 1951 summer season at Newark's outdoor swimming pool. *(363/Neg. 930)*

Over 100 children enjoyed the fine summer weather to splash around in Newark's outdoor pool in 1952. *(364/Neg. 1412)*

Magnus schoolboys Russell Horton (left) and Peter Nutting, Newark Rowing Club's first international scullers, earned a debut with the British Team in the World Youth Rowing Championships in Italy in 1969. *(365/Neg. 21262)*

The Mount C of E Junior School, Newark hockey team in 1951. *(366/Neg. 871)*

Balderton senior school's hockey team, had a brilliant season in 1957, winners of the Pratt Cup losing only three out of 40 matches. *(367/Neg. 4875-1)*

Start of the Notts School cross country run at The Edward Cludd School, Southwell in 1970. *(368/Neg. 22217)*

Dusty Hare, ex-England rugby player, pictured as a 17-year-old practising at Magnus Grammar School in 1970. *(369/Neg. 22117)*

TV's actor/comedian Norman Pace, an ex-pupil of the Magnus School, Newark, pictured during one of his early stage performances at the age of 15, as one of Fagin's pick-pockets in the Newark Operatic Society's 1969 production of *Oliver!* *(370/Neg. 20795)*

Averham village
school celebrated its
centenary on 7 July
1950 with a concert.
(371/Neg. 461)

Mayor and
Mayoress Alderman
A.E. Whomsley JP
and Mrs Whomsley
pictured with the
Sconce Hills
Secondary School
band after their
first-ever public
performance at the
Newark Festival of
Youth held at the
Sconce Hills School
Newark in 1960.
(372/Neg. 8840)

The newly-formed
Newark and district
schools orchestra at their
first rehearsal in 1960.
(373/Neg. 8503)

Members of Newark
Junior Town Band
pictured rehearsing in
1963. *(374/Neg. 12432-5)*

Elston Hall school's production of *The Major Domo* written and produced by the staff and boys in 1960. *(375/Neg. 8802)*

Pupils and staff of the Grove Comprehensive School, Balderton take part in their 1970 production of Rodgers and Hammerstein's *The King and I. (376/Neg. 22635)*

The performance by the Newark Magnus Grammar School of **HMS Pinafore** by Gilbert and Sullivan in 1970. *(377/Neg. 23451)*

Youngsters from the Charles Street Methodist Church youth organisations gave a concert at the Hercules Clay school in 1965. *(378/Neg. 14504)*

Ralph Reader surrounded by smiling Scouts and Cubs at Newark's Gang Show in the Palace Arts and Leisure Centre in 1974. *(379/Neg. 30981)*

Young cadets learning to build their own model aircraft at Newark Air Training Corps meeting at Northgate House, Newark in May 1952. *(380/Neg. 1375)*

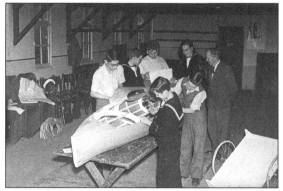

Canoe building, one of the skills being taught at Newark Sea Cadets meeting in 1951. Seen at work on a canoe are T. Thwaites, B. Coombes, J. Rawding, R. Fincham, R. Jater, T.W. Pacey and P. Brewster. *(381/Neg. 1411)*

Radio contacts with Rumania and Hungary were made by Newark Scouts and the Magnus Radio Society who joined forces for the 9th Jamboree on the Air in 1966. *(382/Neg. 16849)*

The Newark unit of the Sea Cadet Corps celebrated their 25th anniversary in 1967. Young cadets are pictured training with a ship's compass at the unit's well-equipped premises TS *Onslow* situated in the Friary grounds, Newark. *(383/Neg. 17137)*

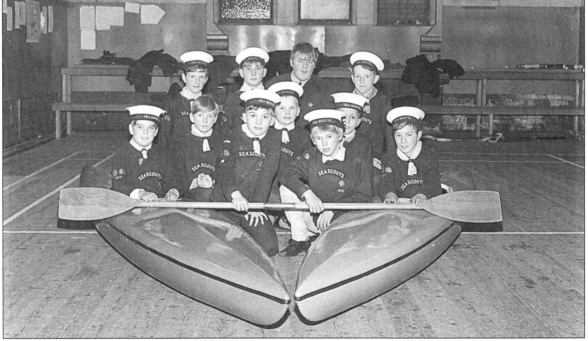

Boys of the 6th Newark (Christ Church) Sea Scouts with the two fibreglass canoes they had constructed in two weeks of evening work in 1968. *(384/Neg. 19970)*

The solemnity of the occasion is reflected in the eyes of Maria Johnson, member of the 1st Collingham Brownie pack, as she lights a candle at the Brownie-Guides Thinking Day celebrations held at Collingham Memorial Hall in 1970. *(385/Neg. 22213)*

Local Guides attended Notts Girl Guides Association diamond jubilee rally at Syerston Aerodrome in 1970. *(386/Neg. 22643)*

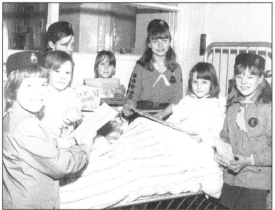

The 9th Newark (Hawtonville) guide company visited the children's ward at Newark Hospital in 1970 to give books to the patients. *(387/Neg. 22210)*

Six-year-old John Hough has a laugh with Smartie the Clown from Smart's Circus when he visited the children in Newark Hospital in 1970. Joining in the fun are, left to right, Pauline Coyle (9), Beverley Myers (10) and Karen Gore (9). *(388/Neg. 22303)*

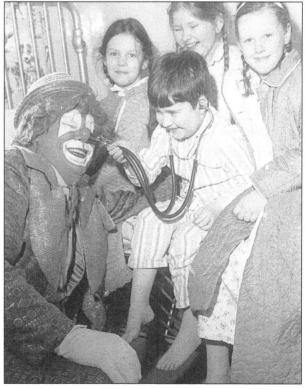

Students of Lilley and Stone Girls' School, Newark speech day held in the Palace Theatre, Newark in 1954. (*389/Neg. 2695-7*)

Duke of Edinburgh presentation in 1970 made by Commander D. Cobb, assistant director of the scheme, at Sconce Hills secondary school. The odd one out at the front of the picture is 14-year-old Stephen Whelbourn – the only boy from 36 winners. (*390/Neg. 22078*)

Heavy snowfall in March 1970 provided the opportunity for youngsters from Averham School to make a snow fort. *(391/Neg. 22260)*

Children enjoy the Punch and Judy Show at the Ransome and Marles Whit Monday gala 1960. *(393/Neg. 8325)*

Budding young jockeys take part in Newark's first donkey derby organised by Newark Round Table at Newark rugby club in 1965. *(395/Neg. 14604)*

Children enjoyed a party at Balderton Working Men's Club in 1963. *(394/Neg. 11423)*

Youngsters fishing in the River Trent opposite Newark Castle in 1968. *(396/Neg. 19285)*

Jack and Jill Wilson went to Devon Park, Newark, entrusting their bucket of water to friend Robin Rayson (9). Jack (10) made encouraging movements of his stick, whilst Jill (8) steadied the net during their fishing expedition in the school holidays in 1972. *(397/Neg. 27408)*

In 1984 water enthusiast Sharon Blake chose the middle of the River Trent as the place for her investiture into Newark's Triton Venture Sea Scout Unit, by Venture Leader Mr Keith Footitt. *(398/Neg. 49631)*

The Eighties

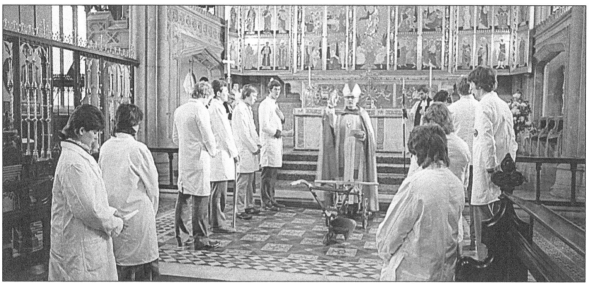

'God Speed the Plough' – the traditional words spoken by the Bishop of Southwell, The Right Revd Denis Wakeling, as he blesses the plough during the annual Plough Sunday service in Newark Parish Church, in January 1985. *(399/Neg. 50355)*

In March 1985 Polish Primate Cardinal Jozel Glemp (centre front) was greeted by hundreds of people when he visited the Polish War Graves at Newark cemetery. *(400/Neg. 50636)*

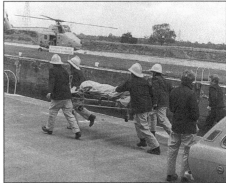

Tragedy struck again at Cromwell Weir in June 1981 when two adults died in a pleasure boat accident. Firemen are seen carrying one of the child survivors from the scene with the RAF helicopter, used in the rescue, in the background. *(402/Neg. 43094)*

Sir John and Lady Eastwood, pictured with the chairman of the Central Notts Health Authority, Mrs Joan Foster, at the official opening of The Eastwood Day Hospital, Newark. *(401/Neg. 52404-13)*

High water in the River Trent in 1981 meant that Mrs Muriel Dyson, landlady of Newark's floating pub, needed a helping hand onto the Wharf Barge. *(403/Neg. 42627)*

Newark auctioneer Max Hopewell escaped unhurt when his Porsche and this lorry took a plunge into the River Trent at Kelham bridge in 1985. (*404/Neg. 52109*)

The *Flying Scotsman* steam locomotive attracted a large crowd of trainspotters when it stopped at Newark Northgate station to take on water in 1983. (*407/Neg. 46631-5*)

The famous locomotive gathers steam as it leaves Newark Northgate station. *(408/Neg. 46631-A)*

During a blizzard in the winter of 1983 this RAF Vulcan bomber made a spectacular landing at Winthorpe Airfield on its way to its last resting place at Newark Air Museum. *(409/Neg. 46525-2)*

Anti-Nuclear Dump protesters were delighted when they successfully prevented contractors from entering Fulbeck airfield in August 1986. They shouted in triumph as Nirex contractors drove away after being confronted by a large crowd. *(406/Neg. 54009)*

ND - #0224 - 270225 - C0 - 246/189/9 - PB - 9781780915098 - Gloss Lamination